TILL NO LIGHT LEAPS

Other books by the Author:

Till No Light Leaps

THE SELECTED POEMS
OF
JAMES MAGNER, JR.

THE GOLDEN QUILL PRESS
Publishers
Francestown   New Hampshire

Library of Congress Catalog Card Number 81-80124

ISBN 0-8233-0327-6

Printed in the United States of America

To my reader
and all who have loved me
and whom I have loved
for all their days
and nights

ACKNOWLEDGMENTS

The author is grateful for permission to reprint poems that were first published in the following presses or journals: *The American Bard; America Sings; The Blue River Poetry Magazine; The Blue River Anthology,* (Blue River Poetry Press); *College English; The National Poetry Anthology,* 1964; *Vignettes of Mid Summer,* (Blue River Poetry Press); *American Weave; The Christian Century; Fine Arts; The Hiram Poetry Review; Podium; Spirit; Tangent; American Poetry, Old and New,* (Young Publications); *Cathedral Poets I,* (Boxwood Press); *Toiler of the Sea, Although There Is the Night, The Golden Quill Anthology, To Whom You Shall Go,* (The Golden Quill Press); *Gethsemane,* (Poetry Seminary Press); *The Dark Is Closest to the Moon, Women of the Golden Horn,* (The Ryder Press); *The International Who's Who in Poetry,* (International Bibliography Center); *Mediterranean Review; The New England Review; Poets on the Platform; Read Out, Read In; The Strong Voice, I, II, III,* (Ashland Poetry Press); *The Back Door; Jam Today; Review '75, '76,* (The Pale Horse Press); *WCLV Cleveland Guide; Illinois Quarterly.*

CONTENTS

From

TOILER OF THE SEA

Sail forth — steer for the deep waters only,
Reckless O soul, exploring, I with thee, and thou
  with me,
For we are bound where mariner has not yet dared
  to go,
And we will risk the ship, ourselves and all.

Walt Whitman
Passage to India

PRAYER AND VISION
BEFORE THE PYRAMID OF THE LOGOS

After dawn, upon the vast purple plains of new-born light
I saw huge, a triangular shape pierce the canopy
    of the world,
Its sides gleaming in ascension
and its shape cast not a shadow upon the world
but a brilliance which brightened dawn.
Its base rose from beyond the ends of the vaulted horizon
and its three cosmic sides converged in a Point
above the arch of dying stars.
And as I stood amazed upon the steppes of earth's
    existence
the sides began to glow and their glory meant to me
in scarlet, gold and fuchsia
the compendium of all the mighty world
from oceaned bosom and himalayic shapes
to cosmic crown of star-strewn skies.
And as I watched, the Point that had begot the
    mammoth sides
became the form of man and bent to me
and I ascended
and now am lost
in the arms of the Form of the world.

LITTLE ONE, TO YOU

You are, to my person's odd creature, my heart,
The earth's bright beauty
    and the reason for laughter,
       — the rhythmed, tangoed kick of this world's
        intoxication,
The belief of renaissance come for me
Amidst the swirling, sinking mass of splintered masts
         and charred spars of soul
Slipping silent to a million-fathomed mausoleum.
You are my belief amidst this ruin,
There is a glory in reaching port, and a warmth
    in home-coming.
That warmth — all the warmth I will
         of this earth's fire —
I feel in the pulse of gentle fires
In the infinitesimal cup of your maiden-hand.

TO DONALD BASHOR

Now the end of that night, and day.
Now the end of dark bat-flights
Unto the mad eye of torn moon
                bleeding in tattered clouds.
Your hammer has swung you sleep
In the quilt-deep arms of the ebon God
Who does not only judge but listens.

(Note: Young Bashor was executed for a
series of seemingly pointless hammer slay-
ings. The convicted man maintained to the
end that he was a victim of schizophrenia.)

THE MAN WITHOUT A FACE

Gutted, tangled — sprawled like a broken crab,
Glorious in enstillment, in encrusted crucified
    entanglement.
Near-dust now, but sometime alive in night-fires
    of high-men's souls.
He, dead and alone in his body,
Seaweed shredded upon assaulted wire;
        without a face.
Far from the reach of our hands,
Entombed in the heart of our mind,
Victorious in forward sprawl;
One of those who fought.

MINIATURE OF LOVE

Awaking from sleep to a room of day
I understood in the twist of a knob
the prolongation of love.
For between the door and frame a crack widened,
And in the crack, a jewelled eye of me,
looking back to me;
I looking into love, and my own love back to me;
My blessed earth in the likeness of the living God!
       My son.

BARTIMEUS

It is a nice day for vultures
and the cooking of carrion
beneath the sadistic heavens.
The wind has clogged my heart
with dust.
I am blind to the world of the sunflower
and the full-lipped smile.
I am crooked and cross-legged,
cast in the shape of humanity before death;
and yet from far off
or deep in nowhere
comes a music — intermittent yet heard
that still makes me aspire;
there is a hand
that still strums the lyre.
And a crowd passes by
and a voice out of crusted chords
sings loud:

"Jesus, Son of David, Have Mercy."

A ROOT OF BLOOM

Honesty is a root of terror
which must grow if the flower bloom
though in shades of night
unseen by the world's twinkling populace
applauding hothouse shows.
Honesty is a root that sometimes splits
preformed molds of earth
and creates chaos in patterned gardens.
Honesty is a root which derives food
from diverse sources:
cisterns, cesspools, fountains —
whatever makes it strong enough
to bloom splendrous in the night.

WHEN SHALL THE NIGHT BE GONE?

When shall I rise and the night be gone,*
When shall I, in this prison of earth,
be lifted beyond the chained and the blind?

You are lifted in the aspiration of your life,
        in the orientation of your being.
Not so much to become but to be
now; your vocation is the life of exercise
in the present — the fissure of eternity.
Not what was or shall be —
These are and have their significance
in the intensity of the present,
Wherein you are impaled the distance
of Armageddon to Golgotha,
for races, dark and light,
for the child and for the man;
The nail of the present is fastening in eternity.

* Job 7:3

22

WITH PLATO AS INSPIRATION

"Life is a learning to die,"
The acceptance of an anxiety
that probes its way towards death.
We are unanchored ships
that work uncertain motors
in the bowels of longing hulls;
Ships of contingency,
that roll on swells
        of unknown deeps
— pitching beneath the blind arch of night
        forward, down, and up.

THE COCKTAIL PARTY

This place is like a mortuary,
Dead men embalming themselves
that they may, later, two-step to oblivion
in a jiggle of smiling desperation.
Pallid face clicks smiling teeth
at smiling teeth of pallid face
powdered for an evening that moves unnoticed
        to eternity.

I do not abhor the Boar's Head
but there are too many dead men here.

REFLECTION'S ANSWER

Are we who come from somewhere
       in tumescence and the womb,
Born from wandering astrologers?
Or does this world, designed and carved,
Give purpose towards a destiny?

"It is your course to steer
not by the astrologer's star nor the moon's opiate
    eye
But to move outward in the chartless ocean-deep
In the sure magnetic tug
of love,
beneath the terror of the night."

THE BRIDGE OF BLESSÉD DANGER
(To the Most Reverend John J. Wright,
Bishop of Pittsburgh)

Perhaps the time has come
when we must look
above the arc of world
and leave to those
who weigh and sift
its soot and rocks
the measurement of aging finity.

Perhaps the time has come
to end this life of darkness
by a death of shrivelled reason,
for it has led Dunois
to windless dawns
of watching birds upon the Loire
before an armored enemy.

I will untrench myself
and dare to cross and bleed
and leave the tactics of defeat to generals
and go on foot behind the Maid.

I will also listen to voices
that urge me danger,
though still in dark,
before the towers of Orleans.

From

ALTHOUGH THERE IS THE NIGHT

DEDICATION

Tonight I am with you, and this is what I am and what I want to be — *cum esse*, available to you in my suffering for your suffering — to share with you yourself and myself in uniqueness and the co-naturality of our human existence. I exist for *you*. This is my poetry, my life, and my direction in and towards God. You and He are my ultimate and sole concern.

I am Jew, I am Christian, I am Hindu and Moslem — I am he who passionately desires fulfillment in that which will complete him.

I am white, I am black; I am prisoner and freeman; I am in darkness, but follow light; I succumb, but forever arise.

I am for you, I am with you, I am in you, I am by you — and if I am not, I am not.

An introduction to a poetry reading
James Edmund Magner, Jr.

29

"Que bien sé yo la fonte que mana y corre aunque es de noche." *

San Juan de la Cruz
"La Fonte"

* "How well I (strive to) know the fount that runs and springs although there is the night."

St. John of the Cross
The Fountain
(my interpolation)

IF THERE BE ONLY NIGHT

If there be only night
behind these world-high walls
that we were told
hide gardens for our breathing hearts,
the walls unscaleable
for feeble-climbing sense and mind;
If there be only night and sleep,
still love has had its birth:
for our loving
as a lark
will sing
to brooding sons
that we would love them still
again,
uncaring of the walls
and nights
forever after slept
in ashen gardens
of the dark.

THIS DAY WILL STAND IN HELL

This day will stand in hell for me
when I, someday, look beyond
the stagnant pond, awakened
by the blackbird's frockish bath,
to the sullen eye of window where I stand.
Where shall I be in that time looking back to me?
If in hell, this will still be hell to me.
Still, dark seer, I hope,
for the blackbird springs with life
and knows a promise in his strut
that speaks of more than hell.

LOVE, MY DARK GROWS DARKER

O Love, the dark grows darker
and I am tombed beneath my ribs.
We are the children of winter dreams
and must breed our hope
upon a pale unending stranger
that is Hardy's outleant corpse.
    O Love, I move darker in my darkness
with the blue-forked gentian
of Lawrencian gloom
smoking in my fisted hand
until Pluto, Nada
or the sought-for God of Olivet
crown my hunting
in clay and thorn
or the inward stars of glory.

UNTO THE OBLIVION OF MY SEEKING LOVE
(For George Grauel)

We suffer in our body the wounds of the Lord;
therefore am I not apart from you
in the lovely darkness
of a panelled den
where the tube speaks
its celluloid unconsciousness
to sterile hermits
of suburbia.
I am naked and laid out.
I am shamed in being dressed by other hands.
I am diminished unto transfiguration
by the object-probing of funereal hands
within the sacredness
of my lately husband body.
I am with you and will soon be with you.
You are not alone in any state,
unto the oblivion
of my seeking love.

AHAB OF MELVILLE,
UPON THE INDIAN DEEP

Tall, dark, brooding beneath the reeling dome of
    world,
His eyes watching the rhythmed, swelling contour
of order and disorder, he does not know.
But moving towards the infinite, the vortex
of the terrible,
Alone and mighty in his deep-fathomed will,
not to be capsized or beached or becalmed
by the bright Starbuck.
Buttressed by his splintered ivory,
deep-heated by the fire of the damned,
living for the harpoon driven
into the bowels of the whale,
that damnèd Principle;
He, never to be turned back,
relishing the sea-grave Dark
upon the back of Moby Dick,
The Archetype of courageous human hopelessness
urges his sail, high and full,
to the outer Indian deep.

IN THIS DARK OF
FOG-BOUND REGIONS OCEANIC

In this dark of fog-bound regions oceanic
and the blinded god that I used to set my sail by
— the holy argus, night, cataract'd in clouds —
where is my peace and hope to seek by?
Where is the shore to point my bow to?
No matter; I will labor,
and wheel my boat with love:
this, the end itself, whether shores or stars
    ever did exist.
We are the toilers of the sea
and this our given time and space,
And triumph be our effort
And love, somehow, our legacy.

LUTHER, THE MODERN MAN, ALONE

Lord, in this evolving night I stand
beneath the sweep of Thy sidereal splendor
knowing that other nights will come
before the new day dawns.
O my conscience is a point of flame
that no man may blow out
and because it burns of me
without flicker from Thy breath
I think it is of Thee.
I do not fear the sea but search,
and if I die in bowsprit plunge
in this mountain-watered deep,
I know I search in death
to those subterranean caves and coves
where I shall surface to Thy dawning gaze.
And so I hope in love
that in Thy mighty heart Thou will receive me
after this long suspended night
of deprivation.

IT IS OUR GLORY TO LIVE
AMID THE DANGERS OF THIS WORLD

It is our glory to live amid the dangers of this world.
To endure the prismed smile of righteousness
from one we thought a lover,
To brace beneath banter
of mindless, frenzied priests
of one cause or the other,
To love in darkness and seek the mouth
that spat upon our face,
To look, then, to Caiaphan fires
where the giant lover monkey-chatters
to save his crawling skin,
And to be lifted, toward the end of day,
in glory and seeming despair
that someone might wonder why
and think in silence upon our passioned dream.

ZERO MINUS ONE MINUTE

The dawn has come
to sleepless night
again
and it is time for us to answer
from the gray, crystal holes
that seem to womb
just northern night and nothingness;
but we are there;
our eyes electric,
our bodies splinters
in bundled rags;
we are there
and we shall creak
our frozen bones
upon that crystal mount
that looms in silence
and amaze the world.

There is no sound
and the world doubts
that we exist
— that we will creak
like brittle crabs
upon that skull,
consummate mount,
into the very hollow of its eyes
that will flash us death
or simply stare us life
and frozen day
again.

39

A MAN WITH THE EYES OF GOD

I dreamt one night
of a man with the eyes of God
and the hind of a pig.
And, as he rooted in the rot of earth,
he would, at times, look up
and his eyes would jewel tears.

AFTER FATHERING SHADOWS

After fathering shadows
behind the screen,
After charismic oration
exploding people to fire,
After sowing the Word
on the tongues of mouths
bearing the hobbled
to mansions of light,
to paternal kiss and the ring,
Who will save the preacher,
the gimp with the golden tongue?

DEAD-MAN'S TOWN

Yesterday I came back to Dead-Man's Town,
to smiling seas of non-involvement
and the madras straightjacket
of industrious anonymity;
into the security of the unconscious
and smooth-shaved greens
and delicious flapping flags
and hollow sounds of balls
whipped into dumb flight
by muscled hollow men
whose voices echo
outside themselves
through tombs of warming showers
and 19th hole addiction.
Yesterday I came back to those I love
to say in some indirection
that I cared,
but their gelatin eyes
followed the arcing orb
to its destiny
in a cavity
below the green sod.

I: MAN, GETHSEMANEAN, PROTEAN

I kneel above this valley of the world
in the sullen warmth of olive groves
that crown the reeling cosmos
and give a festive pinnacle
to the nauseate agony of man.
This mount, this world, this time
weigh in my belly, sick,
and bleed me through the pores of my skin.
My ghost groans in my body
and I am in nausea
with that limping dwarf
— myself-in-man —
who stumbles, aspiring,
to the cliff of Icarus
and is gone.

* * * * *

Now, protean, I stand
as Ahab,
scored, stark and damned,
willing that the sea-grave dark
— that myriad-shadowed mausoleum —
be my oblivion, my glory
my nada-Eden.

Ah Bartleby! Ah Humanity!

* * * * *

43

O God of rocks and deeps and stars,
O God of scars and ecstasy,
I know, though outward worlds abort,
that in my protean, Jungean deeps,
beyond the darkness that the mind perceives,
beyond the struggle of colossal shapes,
in the valley of faith's repose,
that Ahab, long bent upon the monstrous whale,
lies, docile, in the arms of Christ.

I HAVE COME BY WAY OF THE HORN

I have come by way of the Horn;
not through the lush green around Culebra
cut by men who agonized long before
your cocktail-ardor and midnight tangos
slurred to an unconscious beat.
Not through smooth lakes and locks
that open to Balboa and jade-green lawns
that slope to the smooth Pacific.
I have come by way of the Horn,
outside and far off
from silent staterooms
of resting souls
awakened to the five o'clock sitting;
within a rotten skiff,
beneath the arcing waters
and Andean shapes
that gave Magellan's world
its southern form,
I sail on,
a worn and wind-carved being,
far below the opiate breeze
and dance of bougainvillaea
upon the darkened balconies
of Latin kings.

MEDITATION OF A FATHER — 2:00 A.M.

I have often thought of him as a meteor
arcing the Indian heavens,
transforming itself from earth to flame
above the tidalled curve of Asia
until he lay exhausted on an isle in the China Sea
(— the measure of the far, mystic might of him)
— his black hair white,
his face a glorious, golden skull,
his eyes dialing the wonder
of Orient blue,
his soul thronging his body,
his heart still zealing his mind
even into wrestles of death,
his body ablaze
— a cross beneath the pale curve
of searing blue;
O I long for him,
my soul longs to be a Xavier
and race to perennial horizons;
and then I remember
that in my days
I have been such a lumber
to myself,
that His Dolorosa is always beneath
my clubbed and claying feet,
that the Cross of death and triumph
need not be on an isle in the China Sea,
and that I — or someone else
in some other land —

rinse the loins
of another Xavier
helpless in his infant squirmings,
not yet in his mystic might
nor in a conquering mood
in the ultimate parts of Asia.

COME, LITTLE DAVID, PLAY ON YOUR HARP
(A father to his smallest son)

The world no longer streams its melody through my mind
and all its beat is in my plodding step.
So come, little David, play on your harp.

Strength and fire and thronging soul
are palsied memories and pale dreams of mind.
So come, little David, play on your harp.

And Arnold's Dover withdraws once again
and the tidalled ocean palls out the stars.
Dance, little David, play on your harp.

And Endor's witch deciphers my dreams
and life's a nightmare of her blacken smile.
O, little David, dance for your king.

Is all the utter rock-barren strain
sieved in darkness through porous sand?
Sing, little David, sing for your king.

O I will not pursue you in Juda's caves
but clap my hands and learn from you
the rhythm, the order, the pulse, the dance
of this world's syncópate might.
Lord, little David, come play for your king.

O that defiant inchoate fire
that breathes you in my heart

and lights the dampened flambeaus
within the darkened chambered world
is your strut, Little David, as you sing me your
    songs.

Now do I draw strong wine in song
that makes me armor flesh again
to pierce the hulk of the Philistine
upon the plains of Gaza.
So play, so sing, so dance, so strut,
O son, Little David, play wild on your harp.

I AM THE SON OF JACOB

My father is weary
so I must go at dawn
to that place
where he grappled, courageous,
with that huge and agile stranger
who wrung from him
his weary groans of ecstasy
and left him bruised
— all rubied —
beneath the rising sun.
I must take upon myself
the heritage of struggle
and strive as the Western son of Man
upon the plains of Phanuel.

THE DEAD ARE ALWAYS WITH ME

The Dead are always with me
— more living than the Live,
for they have been assumed
to quiet caves of mind
where I do dwell
silent-souled and listening
to the beauty of their lives.

Contingency is the wheel of world
that spins without us
and whirls its fire into spatial sky,
but we are here
too one
to be alone:
the thought and the thinker
the fire and the fired.

IN THE SWING-RADIANT DARKNESS OF
YOUR DARK-FIRED TEXTS
(For Gerard Manley Hopkins)

If you, father, could now see
what your swing-radiant darkness has done
to me, instressed me God whom I cannot see,
lived me, dwelled me in the vortex-swirlings,
in the harlot glory of the reeling world —
her cosmic arms about me
but I, a radiant splinter,
because I ember, live you
in the díaphan dance
of your dark-fired texts.

ARCHITECTONIC

If our eyes light on breasts
without the world as complement,
then we lust.
It is in seeking the bulk in beauty
as sweetness all itself that we sin.
We must long to harmonize
ourselves with all
and see the curve of Degas' girl
as a small loop in the arc of world
that's made to dance by soul and mind.

LOVE COMES TO SHATTER
DREAM'S CREATION

Love comes to shatter dream's creation:
A poem I was to write.
Instead, a white-haired boy,
a tear, his flood of earth,
within his eye,
screams his shattered world,
his shattered toy.
And so,
A wheel to replace,
A tear to dry,
A daughter to reprove:
reality righted
and a dream lost;
No,
given away
for mending.

THE CROW

The crow has my soul
in that wild wood
where he sings his jaggy song
in freedom of his stance and flight.
To the old days does he carry me,
to the wild and young days
where I fathomed eternity
in the blood of my passion
and the light of wanting dreams.

The crow is my soul
and sings, unseen,
his raucous cry of aspiration
— that cry that always signals his flight
beyond the wooded myriad
to outer unseen regions
of the forest.

STUDENT, SACRED WOMAN OF MY HEART

I, student, sacred woman of my heart
or child abed,
will not jostle you
or rape you with the ego's streaking day
or night of deviate longings
but with soft blood-filled
hands of foliate radiance
will unfold the covers
of your hiding place
and raise you to your sleeping feet
and destiny
beyond the shaded window's darkness.

SOME SONGS MUST REMAIN UNSUNG
(For Mary Ann and the children)

Some songs must remain unsung,
hidden in the umbraed wells of mind,
still longing for their mouths
and crying tongues of time
when we, among our children,
are lowered to our room of earth.
For them we have laid away our pens
and given them our hearts
instead.
For words cannot speak the kiss of mouth.

Some songs must remain unsung,
and it is our love
that keeps them coffered
in amnesiaed dust
until
we rise,remembered,
and sing them all
by heart
to heirs of radiant light.

UPON THE BEACH

O take me outward and beyond the sea
where waking dreams from deeps
will find me alone and free,
no more bound by man's nettling voices
and the clamor of crowds
upon the flagrant quay.

O take me outward and beyond the surf
of man's abrupting pride and sounding mind
to listen to the stilly voices
beneath the surface
of the rising sea.

Take me outward to your circling gaze
that drinks the sea from sleekened rim,
for I have come to know
that my soul's love
is only
You.

HYMN OF LAZARUS
(For Dietrich Bonhoeffer)
disciple of Christ
d. 1945

As I sit alone
in the stark and lonely tower of my soul
and see the vast and bleeding world
emerge
unto its writhing present,
I know that He
whose gestation is the birth of light
does not live in Palestine
nor in priestly Pontiff Rome
but is suffering, smoldering still
in the ovens of his womb
that blossomed forth forever
the bloom of smoke from stacks
and eternity of chimneys
that spire
the world
from Auschwitz.*
There my father
gives birth to me again,
and though I have been these long years dead,
I rise again
to meet him
in whose gnarled and bony arms
and eyes as deep as Being
I find the Beyond
within our longing midst.

* Later I learned that Dietrich Bonhoeffer died in
Flossenburg. But no matter. He is himself and all the
Beloved who died in God.

GETHSEMANE

I

Across the arch of thousan'd year
yet deep and simple in my heart's repose
— in the garden of my beginning —
I ponder You
and now, amidst the mist and fired regions
of the Iron Triangle*
and the shredded loins of fathers' sons
— no more to beget mighty heirs
to run strong in their aspiring hearts
and dawns of their realizations.
I grieve in You for the bright generations
sheared from their would-be destiny:
of mothers fondling would-be sons,
of would-be sons piggy-backed upon the wraiths
of longing fathers.
The ghost of this world groans for birth in flesh
but is denied life by carbine flash
and napalm bloom.
Oh how shall Thy great womb gestate recompense?
My heart aspires through the plenitude of my doubt.

II

The wrack of finitude and case of flesh
tauts the eagle's heart
that would work wings beyond the mountains
of this reeling world,
and yet does find the nest of its repose

---

* An area of fierce fighting in North Vietnam in 1967.

and hope of its completion
within the undulate form of earth's splendorous body.
The body speaks of harmony
and this is the life of the singing eagle's mind.
The body is the resonance of the singing cello's bow.
O God in darkened groves
above the valley of the Cedron
what Cross of paradox
have You carpentered for man,
so dark and sweet
so terrible and sublime
that You lift Yourself a writhing slave
upon the tree of time
to play that mystery and that paradox
into song?

III

Somehow through the sacrament of world
speak to me my faith
for I grow deaf and mind-numbed
in the bantering and the brilliance
of the sophists and the wisemen of this world.
Play me a song keyed above unknowing thunder,
play me a song that in silence sings to me
of certainty and of stillness,
of oneness beyond the disparate parts of logic
and the fumbled blocks of kindergarten Fermis.
Play me that song that clues me
of my nature and my destiny
and tunes my strings to sing my freedom,
a David to his lord.

IV

Music speaks the transcendence of this world
and its harmonic mouth speaks your implication.
It wells within our being
singing in the night inarticulate,
not precise but true,
of the beauty of your dwelling and your strength
within the darkened garden
where You played the universe
its redemptive song
and in the sinews of gestate man
who runs mighty of the song of You:
his sap issues from your aspiration
and his heart heaves concentric
with those convulsive beauteous beats
that did prelude the torches of the traitor
and the kiss that keyed the cross
within our souls
forever.

O play the human song upon the
cello of your heart from forever.
Play that simpleness and the vision
that was the shape of love in You
the night you bore me in yourself
as mother.
The night the stars illumed
the burden of your glory.

Play me unto openness
to the darkened garden of long ago and now,

Play me as song upon divinic string
until I be at last
more than my primping self
vain and strutting before the world's cock-eyed gallery.
O Man's aspiration is your testimony to yourself
and man's love is your transcendent voice
in the sullen darkness of his lonely vigil
above the Cedron of this world.

V

O they are a sacrament to me
and my life is in their eyes,
it rises to me as I speak
and the tides of history course to me
through them:
Mankind and transcendent value
not static but transfigured
in all the shapes of them
move into my heart and reverberate
into the music of my inner being.
It is not easy in this grey dome of world
where discursive reason insists on fixities
and the crushing mind of surety
and primping tyrants of academy
press in upon the soul with measured arguments
for God which is not God at all.
It is not easy to lift to the immeasureable
unless the music of their eyes speaks
my song to my heart
and I am on fire
for them in you again

despite all
in deep-sworn vow
despite all encroachment and reason's drownings.
You are my song and my life in my students,
You are the fire of my children's eyes.

VI

Last night I sinned my Lord
and your convulsion was felt in me
up the axis of the reeling world
and in the heart of being.
It was a sin as all sin is
against the Heart of Being:
A falling of love back into
the opiate den of self,
for self is made complete
when self becomes the Other
and burgeons fruit in marriage
with the Other, the sacredness
of all that is not me.
But in my sin and my despair
I felt the dark transcendence of humanity
in the clay of its despair.
And I was opened deeply
to Jaspers' night of passion
that courses through this poor beast's veins.
I did not gain the light
but gained the darkness
and in this darkness
loved the most abandoned of your heart
in my abandonment.

67

Once again, through your convulsions,
You showed to me the wounds
and dark sublimity
of my (and all) humanity.

VII

To that womb, that room of day
the world returns in its pomp and phantasy,
in its strut and jack-ape conquest,
through the corridors of history
time's fool in jester bells returns
dismayed
— back past the torches and the garden
through the holds of your transcendent memory
that mourns and cherishes
the peasant rhapsody of Nazareth.
To a silence and a *kosmos*
that shapes the alpha cipher
and the world's radiant leap
to its transcendency.
If we do not make the pilgrimage
to Nazareth
there is no Tabor or no flight
beyond the boulder-laden
and mountain-cinctured world.

VIII

Lift us by the *stipes* of your divinity
above the cosmic arch of man's debility,

let the *stipes* spring
the bow of its *patibulum*
and so bring flesh
to the plain of its transcendence,
let the shaft of Son break
the vault of winter dreams
and spring us born of Easter
— Born the vision and the dream
that will commit us
to roll the stone of Sisyphus
beyond his darkened mountain
to the valley of green repose
where stars shall be his eyes,
the ciphers of the glory of his being.
For man and Sisyphus were unbound in Bethany
the day that Lazurus came forth,
and we were Eastered
from the vault that seemed forever
to be blind of stars
that became your eyes
the day you wept for man.

IX

My Lord of thunder and the tidal deep
and the stillness of the heart's repose,
I speak through You in your princely darkness
to the morning's early light of Nazareth
and the woman-virgin of the well
that giving birth to You
gave birth to all.

Say, godly woman,
speak to me in all of woman's forms
of that beauty nameless,
the point of all our spiralling dreams
to which in gonads and in *koan* do we aspire,
Speak and perfume the mind with a scent
that is odorless, ponderless,
beyond the ripened fulness of the melon,
beyond the dance of the intóxic world.
Speak still and beyond the concept
to the heart that is beyond the heart,
kiss the lips of mind with that point of fire
that crucifies and exalts.
As mother you are mid-wife
to my thoughts in prayers
as I stumble-bum amid the alleys
of my deviate longings
and the bouncing ashcans of my startling fears.
Lift me, thou woman consúmmate,
beyond thy womanhood to grace
for this cracked-lipped beggar
now sucks the rice up off the sidewalk
and tongues the moisture in the cracks.
O let the stars alone,
I need sustenance,
Mid-wife and mother
of my dreams and longing.

X

Dark Dark God, Dark God, Dark Lover,
Lord of the spasmed world and Olivet,
in storms beyond all creeds and styles,
in all nomadic disparate searchings,
in Chichester lunacy
upon the Indian Upanishad deep,
in sutras and vedas,
in apocrypha and gospel
in multiplied commentaries
I follow,
head-shaven and eyeless in the Gaza
of Delilahed torment, I follow,
in hopelessness I follow,
in the heart of the world's despair
and the dark annihilative acts of our depravity
I follow,
in all our suicidal griefs
and the gay bars and secret stalls,
in the masturbatic phantasy of crucified youth
whose love the world has pushed to toilet reverie,
in the placard lights of the pimping world
and the headlights beeping for their suburban hell
I follow,
in the concrete click of the chic despairing whore,
in tubercular heaves
upon the staring startled sidewalk
and the whirling papers of yesterday's world
I follow,
in the Plaza's strident alcoholic queens
and anonymous lunch in a gilded tomb

and dusk martinis with phantasmal lovers
who speak the words
of their elemental longings,
in the fat woman sexed in a box of chocolates
that she serves lovingly
to her nourished self
in the primal darkness
of her tower suite,
in the buxom swinging beat
of the leggy queens of peel
and the dark inchoate heat
of their enraptured audience
I follow,
in the old roué of Peacock Alley
who sips and primps
the whitened feathers of his impotence,
in the heart of the lonely priest
weary of fathering shadows
of families not his own
beyond the silken screen of his upright coffin,
who must now return to the mad virago
who cooks and keeps him
in his brownstone hell,
in the cubicular-crazed doctoral student
who bursts from books
to daylight and death
fourteen floors below,
in all of these I follow;
in the Harlem blackman's mainstream kick
— the sure reversal of his longed-for freedom,
in the convulsive scarlet nausea

of the fish-eyed fighter
sloped amid the haze and the crowd's dark roar
listening to the count of his distant defeat,
in the contorted trumpeter of 52nd
whose counterpoint, now, is all in his head
as it weaves with the wine and the women
of his cerebral cortege,
in the maddened dials
of the drunkman's eyes
that blaze his fury
for dreams extinguished
fathoms ago,
in the awful lurching midnight beast
that booms the tunnel seaward
to Coney Island paradise
and consummation
I follow.

In the earth's night-flood of cries
of the unvirgined and the fixed,
of the unfathered and unwanted
that drowns me amid the refuse of my own despair
in the rip-tide of the outgoing sea
I follow,
in my dying assertive autonomy,
sacred, and in search of You.

From

THE DARK IS CLOSEST TO THE MOON

And there is the Catskill eagle . . . and even if he forever flies within the gorge, that gorge is in the mountains; so that even in his lowest swoop the mountain eagle is still higher than other birds upon the plain, even though they soar.

Herman Melville
"The Try-Works"
Moby Dick

SOLDIER OF THE NIGHT

I am the soldier of the night.
Alone along the fields of night,
blind the moon in palling white,
outstep the dark into the dawn
if the dawn exists,
for the stepping is the life
transcendent of the dark and white,
no house, no lamp, no chimneyed curl
but only life outstepping night.
My striving is my God
and to his deep I look in dark
and through the simple eye of sight
do I drink my stepping might.
I am the soldier of the night,
alone along the fields of white
I move on stumping unfelt feet
toward the mountained silent sentinels
that loom their jagged horns upright
to gore the dark and blinded moon
that broods its lonely wound of sight
on frozen plains
of all our mortal longing plight.

AMOR FATI

In love with fate at Your hands
this midnight I sit
beneath the sullen eaves
and drenching arms of maple
thinking where night has taken all,
and will, at last, be my muted destiny;
the night, this silent eyeless womb
to which we deeply go
seeking in paradox
the death that is your nursing heart.
Maples, wind and drenching arms of night
speak to me
in concordance of two worlds
of stone and statues
carved to latinate
that marvelous man
who speaks, now, from marble lips,
his Zenic testament to ages,
"Amor fati"
but I, preposterous child of virtue, add
"Amor fati Dei"
for Your inscrutable beauty holds me fast
as did exemplar Zeno and *ataraxia*
hold him still and indominate
at the crest of the arching world
giving law and writing meditations.
But I, Sir, am soft and lyric
and so aspire to Your person
and Your nails
and Your dark benignity

this night
alone,
and beyond all honor.

ARROW, THE DOG

He moves in darkness of the night,
I know because the swinging headlights
told me so
— that swift black deer-like form,
the lithe compendium of the hidden order
and burning life of the world,
the Doberman called Arrow.

How beauty springs
in the sap and swing
of the fluid dark
and we know it not.

ON A STREET CALLED STRAIGHT

Once when the moon held dominion
in the kingdom of scimitared Shalmaneser
and the cobbles of our sighing city
faced the spheric master
that silvered the alleys of Ashurbanipal
I sat in shadow of the light
in the house of Ananias
and heard the tongue of world
toll my destiny:
it would show me how much I had to suffer
as it had the bandy-legged Tarsan wizard
who stumped the Grecian isles and Asia Minor
for the bloodied Son of Man
— and so it has
down to the murk of Marianna deep
beyond the mental shafts of man to plumb
or caissons of mortal imagination,
yet, I know, not more
than some poor abandoned fool of human
who seeks pity from a god.
O brother gibbeted or lung-burst in unconscious deep
beneath the hyperborean lid of world
I sing of you in your frozen enduring beauty
though forgotten by the god of tides.

TO A CHINAMAN, IN A HOLE, LONG AGO

Does that long-alone matron dream
that this, her bed-warm love,
so sleeps — self-graved, ice-wombed
amid the corn-stalk stubble
of the appalling distance
on the frozen face of day?
O father of your people
in some smoking hut in China
in which hunch the moon-faced children
of your still-now steely dreams,
I, your ordered searcher
with a killer on my sling,
do bequeath my life to you
that you might fly the Yellow Sea
to your startled matron's arms
and curl beholden
amid the pygmies of your loins.
But marbled you lie
— and I, somewhat alive —
this rock-white silent day
of our demagogue damnation.

BEFORE THE MELVILLE CONGRESS
August 1, 1969

Take heart, take heart, O Bulkington! Bear thee grimly,
demigod! Up from the spray of thy ocean perishing —
straight up leaps thy apotheosis!

> Herman Melville,
> "The Lee Shore,"
> *Moby Dick*

These mystic creatures, suddenly translated by night
from unutterable solitudes to our peopled deck, affected
me in a manner not easy to enfold. They seemed newly
crawled forth from beneath the foundations of the world.

> Herman Melville,
> "Two Sides of the Tortoise,"
> *The Encantadas*

Let not the sea of erudition unsoul you, Bulkington,
Live you with the wind
to Atuona or the teeth of dark,
your paradise is in your heart, the ark of dawn,
that promises the kiss of archetypal lip
in the leap of its far Jamaican throb.
(The ladies of Lima are waiting,
The Encantadas,
the aging tortoise of the world
with man's scarred rhapsodies upon its back.)
Turn the luncheon tables into tumult of the Horn,
Turn their heads to throbbing coals
and their souls to gods of dark,
rum their brains with ambergris
that they may speak in iambs and alliterate
in the sibilance and the mystery

of his waking language of the dark.
Garrot them, fictively, out from noon-day dreams
and dissolve them in The Great South Sea
that they, again or for first, may hear
the grand ungodly godlike Song
and know the heart that worshipped in defiance,
— to sit, at last, behind the mask
that mysterys man
and know him from the Eye of storm.

AHAB ATHWART OF THE BASHEE ISLES

"When gliding by the Bashee Isles we emerged at last upon the great South Sea. . . . But few thoughts of Pan stirred Ahab's brain, as standing like an iron statue at his accustomed place beside the mizzen rigging, with one nostril he unthinkingly snuffed the sugary musk from the Bashee Isles (in whose sweet woods mild lovers must be walking), and with the other consciously inhaled the salt breath of the new found sea; that sea in which the hated White Whale must even then be swimming."

Herman Melville,
"The Pacific,"
Moby Dick

Not musk borne on lyric stream from Bashee Isles
nor lee of Nukuheva
nor sing of burtons in the hold's dark deep
(though Starbuck brights my heart with reason's
    breathing)
shall tack me from my deep-keeled course,
for the salt of the great South Sea
flares the furnace of my being
and I am all in flame for chase.
O late Formosa, thou beauty of my youth and loins
where in unwounded dawn
did I entwine my arms like vines
about the milk-skinned girls of Taipeh
and wove the songs that wound a wife,
though musk begets the opiate crave for softness
of a breast the size of ocean
and pastel mouth to cool this scored and coopered
    brow of hell,
my manic longing has been salted
(warped the chambers of my longing heart)

and I will consummate my thrust
deep in the bowels of the life that sprung me,
through the blubber mask that mysterys man,
and it will tell me in its tollings
as we descend the southern deep
what stars are made of coral
and the reason for the earth's
vast tourage
to Hell.

THE DARK IS CLOSEST TO THE MOON
(To Melville-in-Ishmael, Beyond the Sundra Strait)

"And there is the Catskill eagle . . . and even if he forever flies
within the gorge, that gorge is in the mountains; so that even
in his lowest swoop the mountain eagle is still higher than other
birds upon the plain, even though they soar."

> Herman Melville,
> "The Try-Works,"
> *Moby Dick*

Do you remember that star-flung night, beyond the
    Sundra Strait
and all verdant dreams of turning back
to rest our keel within the coral arms of Java
— the sable palms of paradise (or so we think of sleep),
when all the watered world loomed as hurtling hills
about the puny helm
and half-asleep you felt the awful suck and trough
— the splinter Pequod half-way down to hell —
and you awoke and read no compass in the night
but only voodoo fires that furnaced faces
and danced our friends as devils in the night.
It was then you said to me (all our worded world the
    dark and sea)
that though in dark and defilade to the lapping light
    of moon
the Catskill eagle soars the tunnelling gorge (as we)
ensconced of night,
closest to the moon,
highest though unknowing
in strong-willed seeking flight
a thousand feet
above the brightening sea.

WOULD THAT I COULD TURN TO DANCE THE
DAUGHTERS OF MY DAWN-TIME WAKING*

Close! stand close to me Starbuck; let me look into a human
eye; it is better than to gaze into sea or sky; better than to
gaze upon God. By the green land; by the bright hearth
stone! this is the magic glass, man; I see my wife and my child
in thine eye. No, No; stay on board, on board! — lower not
when I do; when branded Ahab gives chase to Moby Dick.
That hazard shall not be thine. No, no! not with the far away
home I see in that eye.

> Herman Melville,
> "The Symphony,"
> *Moby Dick*

Would that I could turn to dance the daughters of my
    dawn-time waking,
the singing elves of my knees,
but iron urge and hooded deep
draw me tow-lined
to my hawsered doom,
and though the sea heave the maiden bosom
of my wife-in-mind
I will turn from thought of her
and the daughters of my lyric longings,
for I am bound to murky deep
taut behind the spasmed arching flukes
of my albino destiny.

O the vast and swelling sea
begets the boy in me

* The daughters referred to are Marian and Martha of the
chapter "The Symphony," *Moby Dick*.

and once again I see the Bedford green and girls
gambol in the hay strewn high of the sea-sprung cape
and hear the radiant tumblings of their young lives'
    laughter.
O Starbuck, out-push of God I hope for,
save me from myself,
give me back myself
that I might bank the fires
of my bellowed being.
Give me your hand, sing me the song of your eyes,
the melody of your tongue
— the night song of cradled humanity
at home with the elves of its knees,
the daughters of my sleeping heart.

BOOZE, FORT DEVENS AND ANGELS

I have had the coal-crawling days
picking pieces of my shattered head in coal lumps
from the weaving dry-heave ground,
then dehydrate and dying
behind the burning furnace
until a smile-shine boot should find me
with its swagger stick above me
snapping its derision.

O I have had the crawling days
mind-stiff and strychnined,
zombied in the weeds
with my brush-hook a metronome
for the whore-night's laughter
careening through the cortex of my soul.

But now the children of the light are upon me
and with radiant tousled heads
come for prayers upon my knees
with their cool fish-mouthed kisses
and their mystic fish-eyed light
and I am drunkard once again
but now of pygmied curling gods
and the nectar
of their breathings
in the night.

ON THE WAY TO APARTMENT NO. 1

I shall meet no Veronica
to ply my cheeks
nor woman to weep
or Cyrene to ease the crease of pain,
but only coal-dust dark
to clog my heart
and carom of ghost-heel corridor
to be my anthem
and crown of lamplight
to be my coronation
into bachelorhood.
And I will stand my ground,
an inverse Christ,
in the silent rooms
of Apartment 1's damnation.
There my hell shall be.
And I shall pitch my coal
the best that I know how
as the lord of loss
would have me do.

I SHALL NOT, ANYMORE, LEAD
STAR-EYED GIRLS THROUGH HELL
(Upon Separation From My Wife)

And the yard-arms were tipped with pallid fire; and touched
at each tri-pointed lightening-rod-end with three tapering white
flames, each of the three tall masts were silently burning in
that sulphurous air, like three gigantic wax tapers before an
altar.

> Herman Melville,
> "The Candles,"
> *Moby Dick*

I shall not, anymore, lead star-eyed girls through hell
nor introduce their shivered souls
to Ahab upon the quarter.
O the night for wives should be becalmed
and all cradle of the moony arms
of him she loves
in down of lover's skin.
But I am alone upon the quarter
and the burning finger
lights the mast-end candles
and the ship's an altar
of my intégral
and exulted
doom,
Farewell.

NEVER THINK THAT YOU . . .

Never think that you upon bland pavement of an
   evening's walk
know what's behind
drawn shades of man's imagination
and apartment's night,
beneath a sallow lamp,
within a shaded skull
of one who sits
in deathroom of his dreams
capped and strapped and belted
for his execution
in the singing and unending hours.
That which makes him live makes him die the more
— that love that drills and sucks the heart
as do far off melodies, nursed of ear
which were sung as child
and he did sing till late
to blossoms of his loins,
elfin angels of the night,
that smiled to him
in lips of his own flesh
that loved him and the singing
that fleeced them nightly
to their dreams.
But now no more.
He broods upon the linear type of page
and contemplates a hanging
or a fastened body
upon the meat-hook of reality.

Never think that you upon bland pavement of an
    evening's walk
know what's behind
drawn shades of man's imagination
and apartment's night.

THE DAMNED

No one comes to you.
So do not sit at the window
and read and look
at people
coming off the bus.
They are going home.
This
is all there is
for you.

ON CHRISTMAS NIGHT

Now does the snow fall
and I am alone again
for love again,
without children or person
along the world of frozen rooftops
and rigored laundry lines
and implacable windows
that seal the lamplight burning
and the lyric heat of hearts
— the heave of hearth and holly
and the honey lips and laughter
of boys with candy canes
and girls of piney breath.
Now is that nightmare
of my origins nativitied:
to be outside the window of my family
looking in.
Now to that place where no one goes
but me
out of love
for one I cannot love
in her singular angularity,
but whose flesh I will not crucify
by the nails of those coffined rooms
in which she'd smother
but where I, Houdini-like
do live and awfully thrive
on
and
on

and
on.
But that they be safe
and she not die
is all my work.
O not her, singular,
but in care
and with the fire of the world
inclusive
do I love,
with the storm of Acongcagua
and the whipping wind of horn
up through the Atacama
to this frozen eye of night.
O now am I crucified this night of birth with him
patibulumed between coitus and charisma
with swollen loins
with head on fire
with bellowed heart
and gut geared
to search forever
into frozen drifts of night
and haunt the alleys of the world
for somewhere, everywhere,
the cónsummate dance of God.

FOR MY SON, JIM, WHEN I
HAVE GONE AWAY

I will be there, my son,
as then, in the dark of room,
with you upon my heart,
you talked to me
and told me of the sorrows
of the day
and the feed-back of the world
that migrained your mike of mind.
Though beneath, in the dark of box,
I will be there, in the dark of your room,
the dark of your heart,
and will listen in your speaking
awake in your words,
for love is not bound to box
or dark or room;
it bears itself in your own speaking,
it weaves itself in your own yearning.
So now, this night, abed,
do not be afraid,
for life is thy keeping
and I am
forever
awake.

WHERE DID YOU GO?
(On The Death of Kevin Hurley)

Boy, where did you go
out of this class and world?
Where the electric, the life, the talk,
the auburn dutch-boy hair
that in its going
leaves your mentor
the constant student
of your loss?

WHILE PREPARING "ADAM'S CURSE"

I teach a class and wonder why
I tense and strut and labor
to fashion minds as beautiful
as those intoxic lines.
Why, when the world's full of wonder
and machinery
and bust and heft
do I lope the creaking boards
and rage,
exhilarate of heart
with their dying breaths,
and love them into loving words?

That somehow they be born to selves
And I, again, in their bearing
lovely into the dark
and world
As if some master had streaked the night
with aureate or fuchsia brush.

AS IF A WOMAN IN UNDRESS . . .

The day lasts
as if a woman in undress
would prolong her golden beauty at a window
to call my heart to gaze
(not eyes but heart upon that golden body in the West).

But I am old, a monk in cell
yet not with hope of blessedness
As they who rest at eve in cowl.
I, alone, do watch the golden body of the world
sink beyond the yearning reach of trees
and my abandoned stare.

ALONE AT WOODLAWN
(For Herman Melville)

In summer's sullen green
and chart of dead within my hand
I have sought and found
your abandoned dust
that never hoped for the sop of resurrection
or compensation for love
but has, now, its awful and beautiful repose
in silent immortal defiance
of all syllógic deity.
And now I stand alone, as you,
beside the oak which designates
and was infant when you brought Malcolm here
so young and godly
in your arms of heart.
O man of God beyond all God
and beneath all deeps
I place my hands
upon your unknowing ivied breast
and salute you in silence
of my grief
for the awful honesty of man.

AND LEAVE THE BARKING DOGS TO
THEIR OWN SAVAGE DARK

I do not know,
cannot resolve the umbraed dance
done in shades that obscure the dancers' form
beneath Alhambran portico,
south, where the sun is a torrid mother
and moon a sullen lover
and leaves breathe women
heavy with perfume
and the mad dogs barking
at the lyric gate of time.
I cannot resolve
whence comes the lyric night of dance
and the barking incisor dogs
flashing in the dark.
But I seek the dance and song
and bathe of that river
from whence they come
and leave the barking dogs
to their own savage dark.

ONLY IN THE DEEPS OF SEA

Only in the deeps of sea
where vaults of water bury me
is my form and writhing grace
known in mirrors' concentricity.
Pressure defines our purpose
and concentrates our eye
until in stillness
and the hanging hour
we become ourselves
before we rise
on tides that rinse the moon of wounds
and night
that shades the heart
in silence.

LYRIC FOR GINSBERG

The orgiastic charismatic suffering consciousness of the
    god-seekers of the beat,
the Howl of the mechanized rape of man,
old Teresias of the ashcan,
of the lonely wounded paradise hunters and man's
    unparadised fate,
Seeker of the Absolute in the Passaic of existence,
leaping, spanning, electric, associative, and lightning
    in dance of mind,
this day burst upon me
god-damned, God-blessed from the Sunflower Sutra
and rivered life over rail yards, grave yards, the busted
    church, kicked-cold Christ
and the forlorn face of world
— burst hope amid the stubble of the severed stalks of
    flower-belled existence,
burst from the river Frisco across the earth
and sent me humming to the heart of concentric fire.
This dry-heave morn
have I seen upon pale page a dwarfian Christ
from the temple whip the tyrant Mollock
who umbras the dreams of man
and castrates conceiving mind.
I have opened a book and discovered
an Israelite in whom there is no guile,
a man with hope
and fire at the center of his heart
who moves from cloaca structures
to rivers of spontaneity.
I have discovered a man only bandied before

on the lips of cocktail fops
who accepts himself in his lonely search for the Beloved.
I have spanned the arc of western world
and have come to sit by the shrouded stranger
and my eyes are coals of love.
The fat lady, the stiff, the hung-up priest
the shining nun
are all here beside us
airing their hang-ups,
smoking their dreams
into the eyes of thought
and heart of fire.
I have discovered this hung-over rummed-of-love morn
a man, a stranger, a naked unaccoutred lover of mankind.
Dwarfian but agapic
and hung-up as the Nazarene
and his father Abraham
and his other father Krishna
on the horns of the ripping bull of world.
Begotten there, not wanting it,
dilemmaed there and embracing it,
shining there in absurdity
and singing to a sunflower.

O Angel of the Sunflower
and, through you, all manshaped forms of hope,
erotic and agapic,
save us from the what-end, hung-over, dry-heave
nada-dawn of our morns
and the shivered ditches of the night.
River your lines and reservoir of love

and through all misshapen forms
spring sunflowers from the earth.

The prophets are not dead,
they lurk in the weeds and cough in the ashcans.
God is in Abraham's arms
and Pap Finn's become an angel:
Ginsberg is here.
Love comes in odd shapes
and Christ crouches beneath the bridge.
As a man is, so let him love
for who shall prescribe the forms that love shall take.
Blessed are you Allen, Angel of the Sunflower
and wound of the outcast world,
outside Jericho
but the walls shall come tumbling down.
May stars run rivers of heaven
and the day annoint you with fire,
may night huddle your thighs
and streak you the arrow of dawn.
Shalom, my brother, Shalom achi,
Shalom   Shalom   Shalom

IN THE BLAZE OF DAY

Things come together in the flood of day
with things moving in my mind
from people and from words . . .
The Glass House of Roethke upon my lap
and the dancing bear
taking me away
to the green
and the flow
and the mobile hip
of play.
A professor dreams in my heart
. . . Markman dead
the procession of the dead in the blaze of day:
the static rows of the dead
that I passed before the Triborough
I become
and am nauseous in that becoming,
or is there a leap that flows with the river
out to the sea?
Does Hart Crane live in choired cables
over river-flow
or is all just mold
beneath the rows
before the Triborough?
This spanning glass of Hilton,
these silk-dark woman's legs that pass,
these people pouring corners of their lives to me
in eyes through which I drain
their infinite implication

. . . O my people, O my sons, O daughters
where do you go?
The night dreams the want in me:
Jean kissed my face the night I cried convulsively,
the world in its awful invisibility
kisses me
above my heart,
but what of tonight
when my needs are not invisible?
The crying, the flow, the dead, the want in me
all come together in the blaze of day
when I, alone,
and in rhapsody
look upon the world
that pours herself
into molds beside the Triborough
or outward to the sea.

From

THE WOMEN OF THE GOLDEN HORN

I am the hunter that never rests!
The hunter without a home!
She I seek still flies before:
and I follow,
though she lead beyond the reef;
through sunless seas
and into the night and death.

from *Mardi: A Voyage Thither*
Herman Melville

THE WOMEN OF THE GOLDEN HORN
(Along Condado Beach, San Juan, Puerto Rico)

They come
some sweet and early
wind-kissed of curve
and poised in virginity
for someone's princely seed
to beget a destiny in them.
Some in eve
come alone and wanting
too shy in woman-stem
to ask to be loved
by the ebony latin
that lopes behind.
They come late
when I am alone and dying
the night away
thirsting for the silver in my stance
but numb to the language of my eyes:
to trade all my silver
for their hearts' warmth
babe-asleep upon me,
this dark and longing isle of world.

NOW, IN THIS MOMENT

Do not tell me
the cat
with midnight ears
and violet eyes
is not beautiful
because the river ends
in falls.

Your beauty is intoxic,
a light and song,
your hair
the darkened river of my heart
and singing life
still moves this pen
to tell you so.

IN THE COUNTRY OF NO DEATH

I shall try, this night, with you
to live in the country of no death
that is your eyes and the now and the touch
and the lyric of your untiring life.
I have dragged myself to a ledge
on cadaver heights of the Matterhorn
in the last rigor of my reach
for that point Pennine,
poised and alterior
in its jagged conical beauty
as the all of noble splendor
of manhood height.
But now in sleep, in dream,
I am warm in the night with you
in the country of no death
and I
have entered your eyes.

THIS WOMAN, I CALL LIBRARY

This wonder and the light of shelves
breeds in me a reigning fire
as if the blood were cordialled in a yoga body
— the possibility of life, and thunder
— the shaft of lightning in the heart
that comes out song somehow
from weary pen.
Somehow, amid the shelves,
a woman lurks for me
in all her splendid beauty
poised
in radiance of her stance
and rhapsody.
I do not know how
or how to speak it
but here there is the possibility
of life
— a fertility gives to life a child
for all my generations
when I sleep
up-facing to their pensive light
beneath seasons of my written fruit
triumphant with the dead.

PLAY HER BODY AS A CELLO
(For Wife-Wooers)

Play her body as a cello
with intuition's fingers
upon the bow of song
and tender hands of fire
upon her fiddle shape
and sense the bosomed resonance
of the music of her chambers
as you sweep her singing waist.
Put your cheek against the cello
and play, wild and reasoned artist,
in the throbbing of the God
of your lyric pouring stem
— agapic singing bow —
that has caught the girl in stillness
and musicked her
a woman.

WILL THAT BEAUTY DWELL
IN DREAMS OF AGE?

Will that beauty dwell in dreams of age?
O Lady, do not relinquish your immortal crown
that you may stay with me
in my future rooms of dark
where I, wheel-chaired, dote on
the scrabble
of yesterday's existence.

Stay with me this one belled hour
and dwell in me your tone of heart
till dust.

DAUGHTER OF THE SINGING LIGHT
(for Maureen)

Somehow from ever
in my seed
was sown the daughter of the singing light.

Out from the towers of babylonic splendor
of that dreamic stalagmite city
that birthed me from its heights
massive along the Hudson
and rising to the sea.
Out from the wino womb of ashcans
and the Rorschack alleys of my pummelings,
the vomit of the yellow blare of bars
upon the oil-sick sound* and sea
and in the lonely watches of my youth
and the lyric soundings of my soul
was her beauty ever
singing in the light.
In shivered sleep in pig-mulch
in Beppu's warping rain,
upon the face of Korea's rigored corpse
and in the cold that crystallized
urine in the air
— below all contorted reveries
and weariness beyond imagination
was there sown, my daughter,
your singing in the light.

* The Long Island Sound

119

In the globic arc of wanderings
and in the single mystic arrow's flight
to find its quivered rest,
among the latter years of bells
and beads and silence
and in the lonely tower of my prayer
were you born(e) the eídolon
of all my dreams of beauty.

No pain, no night
no expenditure could abort
your singing in the light
my daughter.

WHEN I MAKE LOVE TO YOU

When I make love to you
(I stand in ecstatic stupor
before soup cans of a supermarket
waylaid by your nape of neck and half-moon curve of
    hair
above the lyric of your ear
until students stare and irate ladies unhinge their elbows
and grunt me to facticity)
— I make love to all.

(I play now in the gardens of the bright earth's folds,
the psychedelic student of your witchery,
sandboxed and kindergartened of your instruction,
a bearded giant and a boob
before the aisles of man.)

(Take me away
to Marquesan night
harbored in the woman of your warmth.
Take me away,
Take me away
from the catalogued
departmental
superstructured
aisles of man
wherein I am drawn
the distance of my life.)

When I make love to you
I find my soul's sidereal mate

the reeling earth
and the laughing mouths and tongues
of boys and girls
and haunts and coves
where, they, lovers throng
thirsting for the fire not found in flesh
but only in the music of its shape and dance.

When I make love to you,
beyond the rows of metalled earth,
I do to Bantu Orphic child
who dances natural in the Congo wild
and turbaned black of Marrakech
and orphaned Inca of the páramos.
Your name my liquid mantra now
rummed in veins of earth
from Port-au-Prince to Mandalay,
drummed the distance of the day
and night from florid ventricle.

The World's gone song among the cans!
I stand a boob
about to push a cart,
for all I know,
down Angel Falls,
somewhere in rivered green
above the Orinoco,
and all the water's turned to wine
and the earth is burning blessed in the leap of day!

Behind!   Before!   Beyond!

ONE NIGHT, WHEN YOU ARE ALL WOMAN

One night
when you are all woman
and blood is burgundy
and passion is a rose
let me spend my love,
pour out my life
in you.

THE NIGHT OF THE BURNING BLADE

I want no wine
for tonight
is the night
of the burning blade
that can be tempered only
with the water
of the wells
of you.

THE BEGINNING OF A NIGHT

Other men end
their meetings with a kiss
but your dark eyes
and expectant mouth
breed beneath amenities
a longing that must be spelled on lips.
I hold you, now, as forever
as when the pendulum of time
is caught in vertical
and its razor shafts eternity.
Now do I plumb you
to the spring that
is your source
and find the sweet beginnings
of your mystery and the dance
that erects the god of Semele
in me.

THIS MORNING I CALLED
MY SOUL FROM ITS CELLAR

This morning
I called my soul from its cellar.
I clapped my hands at the top of the stairs
and shouted into the darkness, "Alleluia!"
For I'll take my Love to the country
and spread her on the green
and if she'll let me kiss her
she'll see clowns and stars
and the dance of me
and my soul cavorting
in its jeans.

I CANNOT BE WITH YOU INTO DAY

I cannot be with you into day,
for I am an old man
full of torments and dreams
of what might have been.
But this night
take me into the hills
of your womanhood
and my hands will speak
the softness
of all the flowers of the world.

IN HOPE OF EVENING RITUALS

There was a woman
who knew me where
I had no knowledge
and waked me where
I was asleep,
in night
where I had no face,
in song
when I had no ears
she taught me
first vespers of the dawn
so now I seek her, other-souled,
that she might teach me,
without a cope,
the compline
of my final eve.

WHERE IN THE WORLD OF THE
MANY-HEADED GOD OF MEN
(Written outside Nighttown 4-15-70)

Where in the world of the many-headed God of men
does she who causes loneliness
live?
My lines do not cull the arch
of the heart's maddened cry
when I, alone, do sit stilettoed
before a winking double
in the awful plains of waning noon
watching in bedazzled age
the children frolic at the bar of time
that grows dark
and soon, Soon
will go out.

AMONG THE CHOLERIC ANCIENTS

The song is ended,
but as I sit among choleric ancients
flipping cards through smoke
and their raucous laughter
that signals
the hegemony of the brute
or when, in night's persuasion,
I look sideways
through the frolic, hands and glasses
along the smooth mahogany
to nothingness,
that strange and coffered creature
beneath my ribs
cries up through the muffler of my will
and the indignant clamp of reason
its terrible loneliness:
for a home
in the dark
of you.

ELEGY FOR MY SISTER
(Written above New York, the day after her death)

When we were shooting baskets, David,
Strength, beauty and all
the fierceness of her youth
lay down upon the stairs
and called it a day,
     a year, a life.

I remember the day
she whipped Ray Markel
for whipping me.
She was an Amazon of loyalty
flailing in the dust
for her little misfit
who overloaded his mouth
        again.

But now all the Amazon
has flowed away
and left me
hung up
above Flushing Bay
and the awful panorama
of the years.

THE WIND BLOWS NIGHT

The wind blows night
against my door
and as I sit, your hand in mine,
before the coals
that breed a frock for winter,
I sorrow and wonder
at the dark stream
that falls along your shoulders
and promises the night
that has wrapped others
in shivered sheets
of macabre bed
and will take you too
away from me.

THE REASON WHY

O, Lady, you do not understand me yet.
I breach not life
or wound in sightless play.
It is not the world's bauble, excitation,
that makes me stand upon my head,
blow kiss, grow faint or go to bed
or die, pained wine,
beneath the millstone of the world.
It is the reason why, *the being-for*
not wandering fool
in anybody's alley,
but surgeon to those who lie
in tented city
in the evening of our Shiloh,
to tender touch
and labor in the night
when fever rises
for those I am still able
for as long as I can be.
It is the reason why, the reason why
that generates my step and reach
until anxiety
nettle me
in Portuguese embrace
on tides of no beginning.
It is a life inarticulate,
a flow,
from where I do not know,
that gives the reason,

that keeps me to it
beyond the heart's
imagined
stroking power.

FOR MY MOTHER

I heard a Paris tune last night,
an organ-grinder's tune
from the courts of Jackson Heights
weaving out of singing trees
as pennies showered from the breathing air,
weaving as a long girl's hair
along the thighs of reverie,
I heard a tune that told me
your beauty would always be
youth to my aging heart.
I remember your song
rivered out of window
as you sang rinsing dishes
on French Ridge Road
forty years ago,
a song of expectation
for your lover
to return.

He will return
though now the dawn's
an awful birth
to you.

The night will come
as Valentino's robe
and your lover
will return
again.

VOICE ON THE TELEPHONE

The tree cavorts a witch
night slips the gibbet hood
and only your voice
now
is dark's redemptive song.

ATTENDANT OF THE GHOST

If you had let me enter
I would have made music
in you
all the night,
but as it was
you knew the ghost in you
and to that lonely shining god
should we all attend.
And I attended,
and did not enter.
And there resounded
as off the gong of world
Wolfe's enormous silence
dwelling into peace,
and while you slept
I lay in burning guard of you
in all my spendrift love,
a counter god
into the dawn.

EAST ON FAIRMOUNT

The world is in despair
as last night
in the valley of my turnings
and blunted alleys of my dreams
it took on its hood again
of absolute despondence
but you and I, now
east on Fairmount
along green-drenched
valleys of the heart
in the dawn along the river
have taken up our life again
in seeking suns
that arc the rainbow of our Soul
aspiring in the meadow
of our beginning and our end.

SATINA'S DANCE

God, this madness, this morning
women in all the cities of the earth
except this one
in which I live and breathe
and hope for a deliverance,
but last night
I saw Satina dance
and the Greco rhythm of her body
delivered me to a Trojan trance in Sparta
and the wild euphoric hour
when she became the world for Menelaus
so that he could not forget
for whom his youth was born.
O all odyssey, monk or reprobate,
is from or to that dance
in nights we ply our beads
or softly suck the neck of Muskatel
amid moon-drenched weeds
along the Cuyahoga.

In that dance
the serpent was all light
and undid the snake about the tree
and Eve became Ezechial
and wove her body
above the valley of our bones
and Herod's transport at Machaerus
brought Evil's head upon a platter,
for she gathered to herself

all the music of the world
and bouzouki and her feet
bore our souls away,
so once again sat we silent
and Athenean
before the burning shrines of our youth.

(SCRIBBLING FOUND IN THE HOUSE OF CAESAR
ON THE IDES OF MARCH)

FOR CALPURNIA

Now before the darkened altar
which has become my life,
In this hour
when sinews are unstrung
by a million ghostly hands,
I look not for nuns
or children
or the light of sanctuary lamp
but to a lyric shadow
that becomes a woman
in all her darkling beauty
and that beauty
all song
to aging valor.

I am tired, Love,
and the valley of your heart
is where
all grass sings now
away from marble and trumpeting
and strut of senate chambers
where, in unlikely hour,
Brutus and the gods
would have my soul.

IN THE SLANTS OF NIGHT
(In Memory of a dear friend's Father)

He comes in the slants of night
as that bright inscrutable angel
that breaches dream with morn
and in the face of the shivering dwarf
beneath the bridge
that pleads the water of your glance
and in the simple and innominate
silence of your heart
that speaks your destiny
and in that Corregidor of man
whose fingers hold your dark and streaming head
as more jewel than first light's infant
and your buttocks as the heave of God.
So, beloved woman, be patient and be watchful
in enclosure of your shower
or in gala fields of light
for he signals
in song from some high window
of some unknown tongue
and ministers the changes of your days.
No longer is he shaped in figure of his flesh
that you may reminisce
in night's phantasmal gallery
but has now become simple
in all who touch you with their light.
Love looms, as he, immobile and unsavage
against the ocean's beating sea,
thwarting night

with its cyclic eye of light,
defying the tides of dark,
saluting day.

LYRIC OF MY BLOOD

You are all children and songs to me
that reverie enfolded scapes
when bells of twilight sound
and mothers put their babes to sleep
when music of their fires is dying into dream
and wives let toll their breasts of night
for men of their labyrinthine dark.
Always to you
in the taut arc of day
I seek my sleep
in that gardeniaed valley
of your thighs.
Always in you
coiled upon the winch of day
I drink my night
of that covert chalice
of your thighs
wherefrom my strength
and the altar of my sacrifice
　　　　　ascends
in the lyric of my blood.

AFTERWARD

You will not know this now
    but afterward,
when twilight falls on sunken gardens
and impotent V.P.'s
totter to the center
of the parquet floor
for a moribund weave
of a music out of reach
and your glass tips
part of a fifth martini;
then, across the lawn,
longing in your mind's own going
and the sun's late swoon
amid compassional foliage,
you will remember and understand
the meaning of our days
— an arc of months
when you were world, inchoate queen
and river of all my blood and soul to me
    and knew yourself
        a woman.

FOR ONE, LATE MY LOVE

What would you have done
with Jeffers
and "the wild God of the world"
that dwelled
in his cavernous voice
his hawk-haunt eyes
and in the great and lonely tedium
of his gigantic hands
that built, in sunward struggle,
the house
on The Big Sur?

ENTRANCES OF THE NIGHT

Committees and carousals are a bore
for I seek always
in the day
amid the irrelevance of party and the play
the entrances of the night
— the mouths of that abode
where eros culminates in stars
seeking in the one
all who ever were
who are
and ever shall be.
There the visored warlock
reveals his lyric angel
and plays a music
of melodic sighs and openings
of an ultimate country,
that living dark
from which we ever come
and to which we ever go.

BATHSHEBA

As David in the day of light
tranced upon Jerusalem's height
or before the bland obstructions
that I must practice for my meat
— in the lyric darkness of becoming night
as David in the dying light
constant is the taste
for the lyric earth of you.
Woman of Jewery
woven, now, of memory
as David's in the trilling night
(drunk of orange blooms
and the naked scent of you)
you have tilled my heart with sight,
your tongue, now, in my eyes,
your walk within my ribs,
your warmth within my fingertips,
your life
and your blood now
to the ends
of my resurgent earth.

SONG FOR RACHEL

When friends have tumbled
into cabs of night
and city's woven
its seams of dark
then the road to Xanadu's
an easy trek
with you
— a lyric tour
through mystic hills
that crest the valley
of Beppu
where lanterns swing
and school girls sing
the songs that Avila
and the nuns of Zen
have sung.

When all is silent
in our folds of world
and we two unfurled
of uniforms
of commerce and display,
then Jacob wrestles into glory
the incipient dream of Eden
and Rachel unwreathes
the shaman's light
and writhes
all
the prophets promised.

MUSIC INTO NIGHT

Red the lips
Red the gown
Black the hair
    and the gleam,
Black the eyes
    into the light
Black the night
    I took you in
and black the haven
    I took you to,
O night the love
    I had you in
and bright the life
    I poured to you
All, the life
    I gave to you
All the light
    I had in me
into black
    the home of me
which was the dark of you
      — dark, your hold
        of all of me
      O dark the hold
        of all of me.

A MYTH

Oh mi amada
¿ cuándo vendrá
la noche para mí?
Para ti, solamente para ti
a esa entereza
aspiro.
Aunque emborrachado con fatiga de días
Yo deseo esa danza
de la noche
con solo tú.

Perhaps urged by the stories of Pinzón and the voyage of Orellana and the myth he created of the dangerous, the far and the voluptual, a man called Diego crossed the ocean in an open skiff and entered the mouth of the river in the last month of the rains. The green of the largest rain forest of the earth had the hush of a woman poised after bathing. (All of this is fragmentary, for I write hurriedly before the world robes itself for sleep. Even now the light of the square has turned to rose, the prelude to its purple vesting and the dark.)

Diego rowed his skiff impossibly against the silt-laden discharge of the Amazon, seen two-hundred miles into the sea until caught by the Guiana current and filtered far into the Caribbean.

In the second month after the rains, he passed Belém, below the influx of the Tocantins and, though weary, was rhapsodized by the life of the world, his friends of the living shore — tapirs and turtles and

151

manatees; the blessed creatures of no reflection and no manipulation, whose call is the call of God with no interruption, no intermediary. The smell of the rosewood and fresh water porpoise were all the diet of the lean body that heaved into night. At twelve, by the stars, he moored on a branch above the dance of the pirarucu and the smiling indolence of the cameon.

In the third month after the rains, he passed the bluffs of Óbidos and Santarém and the feeding arm of Río Negro. He dreamed always of animals and children and heard their laughter counterpoint the toucanet and smelt the smoke of supper fires and felt the dark entrances of the woman's body and the sleep of a man spent from givenness.

In the sixth month after the rains, he penetrated Pongo de Manseriche Gorge and rowed his boat into the ultimate water of the Marañón, mother of the Amazon, three-thousand three-hundred miles from the sea, and entered the land of the Incas, golden Machu Pichu, and then turned South, now on foot, down the Cordillera of the Andes. He did this because they were there and it was his nature to strive beyond human endurance, to outleap himself and know the mystery outshaped in mountains and the rivers, the analogues of Ganga, and in the search be seized one day by the hand of death and in that seizure be absorbed in the song of Vac, the spouse of Shiva. (All this strange for a Spaniard in a Christian world, but the heart speaks the myths of its own needs — beyond prescription or the law.)

The word written, as the light grows dim, as to man's world and his mind, here in the square of the village in the valley of Santiago, cannot utter that man's journey down the Cordillera, upon the awful páramos, empty of all save the loneliness of man's heart and the cry of the Condor who awaits the moment of his stumbling and the beautiful puma who will contend with the bird for the body of his brother. The word blithely spans the steps of frost-bitten feet that moved to the verge of the grim Atacama and crossed it, somehow, with the relentless tread of a god bent on rest somewhere beyond: the valley of the grape, the square of the sun, the well of the child before whom he would sit and no longer be the teacher but the taught.

A year after his rowing against the silt tides of the Amazon, he looked east, through the mist, and saw the frozen point of Aconcagua, the formidable sentinel of the southern Andes, and this was the signal for his climb past tierra caliente, tierra templada, tierra fría, past el puna, even past the páramos and the mild beasts of this world — llama, vicuña and alpaca — to the realm of vizacha and the possessional heights where no man goes or comes. Yet he went, and he came one day, late, into the valley of the grape, to the square of the sun, the well of the child and with bundled feet, unwinding the wraps on his legs and his body, much as a mummy, who still lives, unwraps the cerements of the dead. For this was the geographic center of his world and heart, the world his heart had made. The child was there as he had dreamed, with the well and the pitcher as he had dreamed. But with

153

other children which he had not dreamed, but understood.

The child turned and looked, with the pitcher in her hand and the song began as he had dreamed and he sat silent as in the dream. But the body is the texture of the soul and so, in need, he looked from her eyes to the pitcher in her hand. He needed water. She turned to the other two — the children by her side — and gave each the water for his need, but to the man of the river and the mountains she looked in all her beauty, put the pitcher on her head and moved away, poised, into the green, into the laughter of the children and the chimes of the forest that became the bells of the campanile that sound the end of the day and the fragment I now write of self.

What, you may ask, will the man of the river and the Cordillera do? Will he die of thirst or longing? No. He has come too far to die outside of arms and without a struggle. He will go into Santiago and find a woman without a man and with children he can labor for. And he will rest in the dark of her hut. And kiss the warmth of her gifts. And then, after long rest, after the children are grown, after the filling of her heart, he will go to Valparaiso and buy a skiff and cross the Pacific and, in the land of the Ganges and Himalayas, start all over again. For such is the earth and such is his nature.

Diego,
    El Viejo del Río
        y los Montañas
            5-17-70

From

TO WHOM YOU SHALL GO

To you,
   Old friend,
      In the bleak mornings of our existence.

TILL NO LIGHT LEAPS

Melville, Hesse, Augustine,
they all had the same mountain,
the flora at the bottom,
the climbing through torrid darkness
to bleak day
and snows,
alone among the snows,
grasping,
thrusting the pick into crevices,
holding on till death,
whether it be the penitential psalms
amid the last attack on Carthage
by the Visigoths,
Siddhartha quiet by the river,
or Melville's implacable walk each day
to wharfs,
it all comes to the north face
of The Matterhorn
with the only thing of comfort
the independent principle of the heart
asserting its life
against the unutterable coldness of the wind,
outside home or touch,
still, in sullied aspiration
and crippling age
to keep on
till no light leaps;
their chillblained hands wound with rope
that signifies in death

their willingness to continue
with alterior foolishness
into fate.

ON THE STEPS OF CHICAGO'S ART INSTITUTE

Excited into the day
on these steps of Chicago's art,
not dead papers
of dead mouths
of M.L.A.,
I have drunk Rodin, Renoir, Monet
in one lyric cup of hour,
bought the *Dance at Bougival*,
the glory of a life
for a dollar,
and I will stand with love
this lonely hour
with my heart the only breastplate
to front the tyranny of my Christian past.
Chicago alive,
I alone
in cleave and thrust
of the bright lance
of The Loop, the people,
my awful angst
and the celebration of my soul
for Monet's *Bordighera*,
Degas' *Morning Bath*
and the one eternal step and look
of the *Dance at Bougival*.

MEETING AT ACOLMAN

Beyond pinnacles and towers
of tudor brick and granite
and congestion of committee and program
— without the obstruction which position plays
and pragmatic fix
that tauts life to machine,
we met again at Acolman.
Administrator and teacher
amazed to find each other
in a moment of life
remote from their familiar world
— upon the unadorned earth
of a remnant court,
before the ancient Spanish eyes
of an empty building
that had no reason, now, for being
but itself
and what its sacredness could reveal
to pensive strangers
who handled with their eyes
its altars, choirs
and, perhaps, a cell
where some lone monk took in,
unknown and unacclaimed,
the glory of the world from his window
and more than the world
in sunrise on Tierce.
But what was made more vital in that Mexican
    domain

and yet more important than Maguey, Acolman
or the valley Valasco adored
was that the current of the bood had not failed,
that one man held another,
though in English reserve,
and gave testimony of the heart
to another's presence —
before the grave, despite the heat that wearies all of
    us away
amid hibiscus, bougainvillea and the rubble glory of
    Technochtitlan.

IN THE GARDENS OF THE EMPEROR MAXIMILIAN

Though you and the dream and Carlotta
are gone
from the flesh of the bearing world
— here in the figure of that mother
whose plains and obsidian temples
transcend the gilt abstraction
of the Hapsburg
far to the Teotehuacáns
unto the austere lesson
of your insurgent mentor
Juarez —
you and I and all must remember
that we are given to a mother of divine forgetfulness
of limit,
that She of whom is made
Valasco's silent valleys
and Rivera's people
does forget her lineaments,
the loveliness of her incidentals,
in her triumphant passage
that creates the tragedy of your lonely morning
and the light of the forest of Chapultepec.

HIGH AND ALONE IN THE LIGHT
OF MY SHADED ROOM

High and alone in the light of my shaded room,
above and amidst the rum-laced organics of the world,
the shepherd barking outside,
telling me his day of life
is tethered to a doghouse,
reading Frank O'Hara,
the exuberant ruminator
of the adventitious texture
of Second Avenue,
the women I have loved and long for
weaving their bodies through my veins,
how I am in the dark careening aria of joy!
Celebrant of the muted, unknown God
who, if he were explicit and unmasked
would not be
and the world would lose its face
and fall back into anonymity.
We live in the ambiguities
which, in their life
and awful primings of our flesh
(and wonder of our dark-eyed souls)
make us leap Nijinskis
in the light
until we bound
in one last heroic arc
to the dark hearts
of the waiting dead.

MASTER, SILENT IN GRANADA
(For Federico García Lorca)

Master, silent in Granada
in obscure arroyo of your night,
Master, silent in Granada
pray for me
that she will come
on steed of febrile song
and lave me
in the river of your blood.

Granada,
hide me in your breasts of night,
your fields of wheat,
folds of vine
— lyric heat
of your olive groves
and the moon hung silver
asleep with wine —
that I may come to sing again
the songs of sensual silence.

Master, silent in Granada
beyond obscure arroyo of your night
Master, singing in Granada
sing for me
that she will come
on steed of rising song
and rinse me
in the river
of your blood.

FOR YOU, OLD FRIEND, IN THE
BLEAK MORNINGS OF OUR EXISTENCE

Let us give ourselves in our deprivation
to those who will receive our love,
not sorrowing over attachment or loss,
but to the world, our children
and the old man upon the stoop
nauseous with his morning diaphany
of muskatel.
Let us, old friend, not be undone by our aloneness
and the ghost hours when the saturday night special
wants entrance into our dreams.
We will not dissolve our hearts
in the woods behind the house
but give ourselves to all who need us
and will absorb what we have garnered
from the weeds, the moon, the Cuyahoga,
the bleak mornings of our sickness
and the eyes we have for paradise.

IN A SUBURBAN RAILWAY STATION

I sit in a train station
in a lyric suburb
beneath the flaunting trees of fall,
reading the shaman Duncan,
dreaming of the time you will come
and your eyes will be the region
of my life again
— that country where no light goes out,
and now
the trees are all afire
for the look of you.

I SIT IN THE DARK . . .

I sit in the dark
of a tree
of no fruit
and a mad woman
screams the wind.

ALWAYS ACROSS THE AISLE . . .

Always across the aisle
    amidst the adventitious bump
of mid-night or rush-hour subway
she sits,
the compendium of all the beauty and maya
of the world
— that face, that form that makes the mind wonder
if light and rest can be had.
But we all know
that in the room where two endure each other
the form and face fall to fragments
and the witch is born out of dream.

FOOL OF BEAUTY

After the nightmares
    and catastrophe
I see her coming again
    in different shapes,
At evening, over the rim
    of a Daiquiri
I see her face as a flower
    that will enclose me
In her house of madness
    again.

FOR THE GARAGEMAN

I am here.
I await you
as Gatsby
of shadowed pool
that day
when the trees
threw down
their hair
and the world
in its tragic wonder
gave up its body
to the light
of the finally undeceived.

LONE TO THE WIND

My boy
without a shirt
appeared
a pale bird
at the kitchen window
signalling his brother for food.
I have sought him
over the streets of my heart,
my life skewered
in his flight.
How shall I resolve
the leaves of summer green
with his loneness
to the wind
without a shirt?
Where is he
for whom my heart dies?

YOURS

Twenty years from now
on some tenement fire escape
or lawn swathed with razors
you will be reading these words
as dusk wanders into rose
and you will love the world
because of ambiguous light,
and my life
will be your blood
in that moment;
that's what it will take
— my dying life
yours
in a summer evening in July
and the sky
wondering rose
into dark.

"JUST SING, DEAR LOUIS . . ."

"Just sing, dear Louis. Unfortunately, I can hear
nothing; I only want to see you sing."
I think I see Crowe before me
     as he would have been in off hours
     in the library
     reading the light of the world.
How shall I collect all reverie
     all song and shadows?
Only by this contrapuntal look, this light
     of word
that gathers an Indian woman
before the fingering fire of her dreams
vanishing in a crevice of The Sierra Madre
— all my journeys and all my reveries
     I bequeath in their disparateness
          to you
— the dying Beethoven seeing the singer
     he could not hear,
my dead teacher at another table,
the Indian woman that recurs
     at the height of day —
All these, in their splintered sway
     I bequeath to you
As he to his beloved Karl.

The chalice of the day
    is tipped for you
Despite the dark,
    Drink
the green, the light
— O the light of all prancing things!
Tulip! Long-stem!
Blade unsheathed
on sleep-down lawn,
drink the day
— the woman
that you are
and will be
until the leap
has gone
from earth.

WORLD IN FALL

Reading Montale,
and it is happening again,
the curves are flowing golden
in the waterfall
of the world.
As he, I am taken
in her seductive swing
and scent
— chestnuts, smoke and apples,
the erotica of her simmering grace.
Heaven is vertical
in her enormous shedding.
I shall be like Montale.
I know the ferry does not come back.
But I adore the river of its going,
the autumned icon of her splendored life.

FOR CÉSAR VALLEJO

That autumn evening
    when you lay down
with rain and leaves
    upon your face
did Miguel, your elusive angel,
    come for you
triumphant from the years
    of hide and seek
as, for a moment, light sifted
    not from Notre Dame or Sacre Coeur
but from the silent eternal reaches
    of your heart
and the radiant creatures
    of your veins?

— The bells of Santiago
    are ringing, my beloved
    and Ma Ma is calling again,
Miguel and I are wiping your face
    and we will bear you home
        to the Incan aria
        of her prayer.

Listen! The tree toads are singing your return
and the moon   and the night   and bougainvillea
    are enfolding your bones
        for sleep.

TO WHOM YOU SHALL GO

"Poets are the unwashed saints of the world.
   They are not immaculate; they are aware."

When it is too dark
      for anyone else to see
and you stink so
      no one else would approach
Take your body and your soul
      beneath the bridge.
There is an old man there
      who will keep you warm
with the fire
      he has built in a garbage can,
and he will open his deplorable raglan coat
      and let you in
with all the other creatures
      of his unwashed skin.
He will not edify you
      he will just listen
to your dreams
      and the knocking of your heart,
Then rock you to sleep
      as your mother would
amid the eternal snow.

177

GARNER AND THE KID OF 52nd

I've been waylaid by a newspaper.
I'm going in to play your music now
to resurrect melodic pyramids.
In the beginning
on 52nd
I stood in doorways
and saw you roll your eyes
and create a music
that drove the angels crazy.
Condon, Spanier, Davidson
Teagarden, Wilson
and you
— these were the angels of my paradise,
and I gave all my silver to see
Graziano at The Garden
and you play light
with your fingers.

Now pyramids will strut forever
fire, life and day.

BE PATIENT WITH ME

Be patient with me
I am, as my dead brothers
    dying with light upon their lips,
    searching the corners of shadow
for one
    for whom   a guitar sings
the days and nights
    of a friend

        always stepping
into darkness,

        in whose touch
a sensuous light,
the singleness of sight.
I mean
    that in my improvisation
    I promise nothing
but the now of my deepest touch
the flame of my fingers
the mouth of my heart
and the sublime impermanence of twilight.

LOVE NOW ALWAYS SINGS THE LIGHT
(For Helen and Nikos Kazantzakis)

How love so sang your letters
        from Gottesgab,
how love haunted her at Salzburg
until, beyond Mozart, Zweig and spires
you were both one angel
in each others arms
as trees sang their morning light.
How love too was lifted in the arms of light
when she placed your dying hand
upon her head to bless her,
and how love now lives
in the arms of night
and all the reaches of the world,
in darkened rooms and corridors
where someone there reads your letters
singing out of phrases
— enfolded readers rise now
and walk the avenues of morn
into the blessed and sacred day
fearing nothing, hoping for nothing
but being free   to be
their own sublime exception.

RESPONSE TO THE LORD OF THE SUR
(For Robinson and Una Jeffers)

I sought to write in blood
          of more turbulent hours
a poem to you, Dark Angel,
to suit your crimson soundings,
but I do not know now
if the effort will abort
from light
— the shaft be
too sheer,
the thought be
without the flesh and blood and bone
that needs to be
a poem.
But out of the night of my orphic cross
I start and say
that the idea, my lord,
is to be
creative
from the center out
completely.

Looking back to lyric interludes
woven through blood and pain,
would you not have chosen
your dearest soul of soul
before the hawk or cat
or any facet
of the majesty of indifference

181

— she "more beautiful than a hawk in flight,"
for whom you wept
on towered stairs to sky
every evening of your life
thereafter?
We, dear lord, are the only arms
          of the armless God,
for we do something it cannot do
in all its wild and tidal power
— rest her dying head within our arms
and kiss her dying mind
into realms of peace.

Did you not celebrate
the sons of both your blood and light
as you held them to the stars
and called them names
out of night and beauty?
Would you not have died
for the God of their eyes
more helpless and compelling
than the falcon's convergent stare
or the immortal obdurate indifference
of the stone?

Creation, falconer, is more than
pain or blood or stone.
It is also the enduring act
of who we are.
It is the tenderness not shown
by "the wild God of the world."

It is reflection that advises
children in the night.
— An effort and a reverence
from the center
completely out
to cormorants
kinged upon the sea
and scallops chafed of surf
unknown to all
but we,
in this interlude
of our pencilled hour,
until our bones become
what they are
in the great enigmatic arc
of the universal tide
that thunders as it sings
its enormity and fragility
in the boulders of the sun
or in the iris
of your passing articulate angel
now celebrant with you
in careening birds,
symphonic turbulence
of Pacific sea
and the ineffable mimetic stare
of flowers' thirsting faces.

ANGEL

Angel, Angel
I am dying into you,
silver sparrows
are raining from your eyes
and rain is harvesting the night,
your well has blossomed lips
breathed the fragrance of its fire,
now, Angel, I am dying into you
dying into you
all my light,
dying into you
dying into you
and I am now
a single singing arrow
silent in its flight.

LADY OF MY NIGHTS AND DAYS

On this day of light
when you will come to me,
somehow Manet's Dead Toreador
comes also to my heart.
It is my death
that is near.
(Near always to those who know of life
and the hour of its beholdment.
Lorca's bed was always light
beneath whose rumpled fire
night fingered its elegy.)
Manet's Toreador,
lyric resolution of a life,
comes to me
and is my death
but this death gives entrance
to what I want to say to you:
I am grateful
for the little while
I have with you
before you pass from me,
Queen of the moon and jasmine
and all the rivers of the night,
— before I pass from you,
Lady of my nights and days,
Lady in need of whom I was
even as I crouched
for light
in incarnadine cave,

Lady in whose person
is all my heart knows
that woman is,
I will be silent now
and just amuse you
(above my heart's convergent fire)
in the little while
before the trumpets sound
and I am arced
on the horns of the moon.

EVERYONE, EVERYONE . . .

Everyone, everyone,
no one is left
but the night.
Everyone, everyone,
nothing is left
of the light.
My life has always been,
after the mountains
and frozen moon,
a gearing
for the final approach
with no field.
Everyone, everyone,
no one is left
but the night.

TO BE GRATEFUL FOR THE LIGHT OF DAYS
(For One Late My Queen)

To be grateful for the light of days
amid nettles and the coursing river
that unfolds its labyrinthe
and wide embrace
though figures wait in ambush.
To be grateful and to be worthy
of giving love
to those who are our blessed charge.
To be worthy of life
which is beyond our good or evil
which is only itself
which is innocent
of our turmoil, our slander
and our indulgence.
To serve it
as our innocent queen,
to give back life
as long as its strength
is in our blood.
To transcend ourselves.
To be grateful for the light of days.

IN MONTALE'S GREENHOUSE

You are with me
in this hour suspended
beneath Montale's lemon trees
which are light
that kisses the mind.
You are with me
in this light
that washes our wounds
and in this hour
that promises a generation
or, simply and supremely, itself.
And I give you
the light of my body
and I hope for you,
from the center of the life
that begot you,
all that is a blessed possibility.
— Beneath the light of his lemon trees,
in this hour of his greenhouse,
in the green world
of his mind.

LIGHT FALLS

Light falls from air
and music from the grace of trees.
It is happening again,
it is always happening,
and there, at the center,
as in Feurbach and Montale
and all the other crests
and convergences of fire,
there is you,
past secrecy,
words and thought.
Only caught in flight
within the fuchsia lightning
of feeling.
O light of my profound inadequacy!
Speak once
and illuminate the valley.

FOR ROBERT LOWELL

I have always been with you
in your net of dreams;
the enormous sorrow and attrition
somehow breaking into light
in words upon the page.
Now we ride, as light dives
into dark
amidst towers
of your appointed city
where Liz
waits still,
her eyes the aperture
for the enclosure of her being.
Past Hooker's statue
and the West St. jail,
Madaket and the aspiration
and demise
of all on cosmic Pequod
borne with you,
your apotheosis, also, in your ocean perishing;
one, now, with Warren Winslow,
Delmore, John and Randall
— brothers of resonance
and nettled glory:
marginal, now, in the world's memory
but becoming deeper
and more relevant
as pages are turned
in lonely absolute rooms.

The bottle is still half empty
and the enormous censer,
ashtray of your anxieties,
signals the beginning
of your obsequies,
and I would bend,
burning surrogate comforter,
as Sexton to John Holmes,
to bring you, at last,
beyond the turn of the river
and all erupting surf
to sleep
that has always longed to wake
beneath the turmoil of our dreams.

NEW POEMS

THE AWFUL SAVIOR

The other night
I stood in the garden,
the coil of man for you
unreleased
and I became the conductor,
in vital residue,
of all the world's
Golgothan lightning.
His hanging time was but three;
mine, a night, a day, a night
of sowing grass, planting bushes,
reading Lowell's anxieties
and writing to my students
on margins of their lettered beauty,
until near midnight
of the second day,
amid filled ashtrays
and my doubled body,
the earth opened
and wine swallowed torment
in despair.
I became
my own lover,
Narcissus
my awful savior.

O CARO MAESTRO

(In Memory of Aldo Moro
and for his wife and children)

I am ignorant
of Via Trionfale, Tre Ochette
— light that inhabited gardens
and children cradled
in the calyx of your soul
amid turmoil of chambers,
contests of cabinet
and the constant binding of Italian wounds
with delicate fingers.

I am ignorant
of Bari and Maglie
and hands held out again
in the country of the poor
— Christ
of the vineyards
of the South
— his face still imploring
from Taranto and Brindisi.

I am ignorant
of the last isolate hour
upon that terminal beach
and the sky, the suffocate envelope
of all dreams
— her arms again, the garden again
and the children

— the silence of the chalice
held in morning
in radiance
of more than eyes or hands.
I am ignorant
of that despair beyond despair
— the ironic culmination of life
into Life.

I can only do this
in the futile love
I bear you.

Oh that love might bear us all,
even bodies of closed trunks,
beyond Torrita Tiberina,
to gardens, arms and children
(O Caro Maestro!)
of our ultimate afternoons.

one
night
a
but
ter
fly
and
a
lo
co
mo
tive
cop
u
la
ted
and
here
i
am

QUIET THE EYES OF PARADISE

Poor Melville: He was determined Paradise existed. So
he was always in purgatory.

> D. H. Lawrence,
> "Herman Melville's *Typee* and *Omoo*."
> Studies in Classic American Literature

"Therefore I pray God that he may quit me of god."

> Meister Ekhart
> Sermon 28

Quit me of Melville, of Christ, of God,
Quiet the eyes of paradise,
the awful voyage to receding isle
in the torrid evening of our Golgotha,
let us rest a while:
Acceptance of contingency
and the sacred erring self,
worship of presences
as they be
— "That ant is mine,"
said Schweitzer to a friend at table,
and every mystic implication
and the world
is in the touch
of one finger to another —
fracture of grandiosity
and Promethean image,
(Let the turn-key and scrivener
of our self-punishment
and the infant tyrant of omnipotence
die of our rejection.

Ahab was not real and Nietzsche died of syphillis.)
Light and dark
of the fluctuating passage,
presence
that is now
not paradisal.

I eschew nothing,
but for now
acquit me of them:
Night of Olives,
Lord of Tides
and the drawing moon
with ethereal mask,
pale and isolate
of my skies
— acquit me of her
also;
foreboding tenor
of my days,
fruit of my deprivation
— let the Cross
be turned to bird.
I am not a god
nor you,
but a man of all my past
and present
becoming who I am,
and there is no archetype
that hangs solid in our skies
unwashed, unwarped

by the rains of time.
Come,
let us make our peace now,
compassion for ourselves and others.
Refuse the gods
that we may give birth to selves.
(The children and the birds arrive at twilight
and rabbits leap in nestling light.
I have seen them in their games,
their gay reality
from my monastic porch.
I have seen them
and they bless me
in their life
— innocence in spontaneity,
life unto radiant lineament
without lust or savagery:
the world's blessing of itself
before the folds of sleep.)

Quiet the eyes of paradise,
acquit me of all gods;
let us rest here awhile
below the mystic porch,
a finger to our lips
as a doe, lifting her head,
startles our hearts into silence
— presences of the real,
unfrocked dignity of the earth;
our hands are folded in silence,
our eyes are given their sleep.

Quiet the eyes of paradise,
Not even the bells, now, of Nara;
cover that picture on the wall,
The Girl With Orange Gown;
she does not await me;
it was my heart only
that gave her projected life;
she is but a girl who lived and died
in her diurnal beauty.

Quiet the eyes; quiet the heart,
quit me of all
but the actual
and love
forever
attendant.

FAITHFUL UNTIL NIGHT

Friend to my heart
as Ruth
who came, unclaimed,
from another country
into untended folds of my fields
and asked the cover
of my cloak,
in how many fading hours,
vortexed glooms
have I sought
the simple nurture
of your gaze.

Be with me
in the fields of light
which your person, only,
signifies
and sows,
and I will be,
as Boaz,
faithful until night.

THROUGH THE LIGHT OF YEARS

(In Memory of my Father, James E. Magner,
born February 24, 1898; died February 19, 1979)

> I suppose, Dad, it is out in the garden
> I would encounter you,
> not in the shades
>   of the isolate house
> where my heart seeks your counsel
> in confessionals of its corners
> and resonances of its silence
> — it is here, with brush in hand,
> painting the old love seat
> after so many years
> — the one relic I have of
> the gardens of Eastchester morning;
> It is here with the lordly poplars
> and trees and bushes I could never name
> as lean and loyal and recalcitrant
> I helped you on Saturday afternoons
> before my midnight gambols
> at Rudy's Barge
> and labyrinthine ways
> from New York cops;
> It was here you taught me resentment,
> but, finally,
> the enduring, convoluted
> song of soul for you:
> the patience with roses I hated
> — the lime, the bonemeal, the mulch,

all such trash
        for a boy wild of heart
and loin.

But now the poplars bend, the locust tree
is a gloried jungle, and the rose of Sharon, now,
my only mistress,
and I am about to do
what I never thought I would
— weed the beds of roses
that never will stop blooming
though storms and winter rape them
                through the light of years.

LETTER TO A WRITER

I see you, swimmer
of the rip-tides of dark,
you arch your nacre stroke
to come upon the beach, at last,
the beach of body, Oh sensuous Platonist
of remembrance,
in which you tongue the radical limit of death,
the torque of life,
the ambiguous sacrament
of the actual and the empyrean,
back into the dark cove
of lost mother,
the mouthing of our origins,
our gardens and our sleep,
cradle of our destruction
and our illusion,
nurse of our wounds
by her breasts;
Oh do we all
as lecherous, needing infants
seek out that soft island
in our thrashing plains of night
but shall we realize
in our urgent stroke
that our life is not in her but in us;
in our awful limit,
the door to birth:
despite our "sickness unto death,"
despite the wound driven past the membrane
of our souls,

so that we are always Jacob
upon the plains of Phanuel,
limping from our wrestling
with our ghosts;
despite the horror of nothing
and our hound's awful howl of fright,
do we stroke no longer
to the beach of our illusion
but walk upright in our limpid state
and, in this acceptance
and calm will to foster life
in whatever face, whatever flower,
whatever night,
the knife to skewer our intent,
can we still whirl our deplorable sling,
though lightly loaded
by our ragged flesh
against Himalayan possibilities.
But all of this, I know,
has the radiance
of cadenced inflation,
yet let us take all mythologies
as our diet,
all phenomena, meat
ingested to our blood
and excrete the rest.
Because of weariness, now, dear man,
let me end
in remembrance of a speaker
of a Jewish myth
that gives the reasoned resolution of my thought,
"Blessed is the man that labors

and is content
for his life shall be made sweet."
(In our labor is our love
and in our love, our life.
This is our redemption.
Despite whatever, all.)
This I wish for you and yours
for all your days and nights.